MUSIC MARKETING USING TWITTER TO GET 1000'S OF REAL TARGETED FANS AND SELL MORE MUSIC, SOCIAL MEDIA PROMOTION FOR THE DIY MUSICIAN, (INTERNET MARKETING, DIGITAL MARKETING, PROMOTION TECHNIQUES, MUSIC BUSINESS, MUSIC INDUSTRY, INDIE MUSICIANS, WEB MARKETING)

Table of contents

Introduction

I want to thank you and congratulate you for downloading the book,

"Music Marketing : Using Twitter To Get 1000's of Real Targeted Fans and Sell More Music, Social Media Promotion for the DIY Musician, (Internet Marketing, Digital Marketing, Promotion Techniques, Music Business, Music Industry, Indie Musicians, Web Marketing)".

This book contains proven steps and strategies on how to effectively use twitter to promote your music and gain 1,000's of followers.

Social media is one of the most powerful tools you can wield in today's day and age. Having a direct link to your fans allows you to craft a stronger connection with them.

Social media can also be a great promotional tool. Your video can be shared all around the world and get in front of people you might not have access to otherwise.

In this book you'll learn how to target a large number of followers on twitter who will already be interested in the kind of music or product you're creating and take your career to the next level.

Thanks again for downloading this book, I hope you enjoy it!

Please leave a review if you find this book useful. I'd really appreciate it.

:)

Chapter 1 – Twitter Basics

Setting Up Your Profile

Head over to Twitter.com and we can begin your social media journey.

This is the first step towards online domination. Here are a few things you'll need to make this happen.

1. Two High Quality Photographs

2. A Short Bio

3. Links To Your Website Or Other Social Media

Before you start putting your profile together have a bit of a think about branding. This will be your homepage on twitter so think about what you want your followers to see when they come here.
Do you want it to appear sleek, artistic, grungy or cool?
Profile Photo – Pick a striking photo. Ideally a face shot as these tend to get more follows than logo pictures.

Header Photo – This photo can get stretched out of focus so make sure you put in a high quality photo or hire someone on fiverr.com to edit a photo to fit the banner. This section is a good place to put a logo or album artwork. It provides a nice back drop to your main photo.

Bio – You only have a few characters here to make an impact so choose your words wisely. Poorly written bios can send potential followers far, far away without a hope of coming back. Make it short and sweet with some key points.

1. What Kind Of Music You Make

2. Any Information About Music Releases Coming Up or Out Now

3. A Phrase About What Makes You Unique

Other Social Media Links – Make sure you add links to your other social media links. Some people use more than one social media platform so add the links and cross promote.

Tweeting

Twitter Keywords and Concepts

Tweet - A tweet is a post of 140 characters or less that will appear in people's news feed. It can contain photos or short videos and is the main way people connect and communicate on Twitter.

Hashtag – This is one of the most important components of twitter. This allows you to connect your posts to people who are interested in the words or topic you hashtag.

For instance if I was to write '#electronicmusic' in my tweet then people who search for and are interested in Electronic Music will come across my tweet and hopefully give it a like, retweet it and even follow me.

Retweet – This is when a user shares another user's post on their home page. Retweets will give you further exposure on Twitter and boost your chance of gaining more followers.

Twitter Handle/ Username – This is your name on Twitter. Sometimes the username you want may be taken so you have to choose another one. Try and get it as close to your real name/band name as you can.

On your bio it will be shown as '@*Then your chosen twitter handle*'

E.G. @bookbub

Mention – A mention is when a user tags another user in their tweet using their twitter handle.

E.G. 'I just want to say a big shout out to @lisadaynes for all her support.'

Lists – These are ways of organizing your incoming tweets. You can sort user into to different lists and view their tweets accordingly. For instance if you follow a few reviewers you can put them in a list so you can always keeps tabs on them and not have their tweets getting lost in your general newfeed.

Notifications – These are little alerts that pop up when something relavant happens regarding your account. This includes new followers, retweets, likes, mentions or when you're added to a list.

At the top of your screen there is a tab saying 'Notifications' and numbers will appear in the tab when new notifications come through.

Trending – When something is trending it means there's a particular hashtag that is being used quite a lot currently. If you use a hashtag when something is trending then you will be able to capture much more people's attention, so watch out for what's trending on the left side of your newsfeed.

Direct Message – A Direct Message (DM for short) is a private message between two users of 140 characters or less. DM's can only be sent if a user follows you.

When To Tweet

If you compose a great tweet and post it but it's 1.30am in the morning. No one (in your time zone) is likely going to see it.
Commuting hours are great times to tweet during the week. 8-9am and 5-6pm.
On the weekend it's a little different. People check their phones more often so it's up to you to experiment but midday or evening are good times to send out a blast
Now if you have fans in different timezones then you'll need to account for the time difference. Either wait up and send them manually or you can schedule them which we'll cover later on.

Who To Follow

As a general courtesy following someone who follows you first is good practice. Some people only follow if they think you're going to follow back. If your followers way outweighs the amount you're following then users might be less likely to follow back.

Also follow interesting people within the music industry. Whether it's someone from within your genre, a music blogger or an event night. Doing so will give you lots of relevant and interesting information you can share on your twitter to gain more exposure and followers.

What To Tweet

1. New music, videos or photoshoots.

2. Behind the scenes clips of studio sessions, tour bus stories.

3. Gig Information or Gig Footage.

4. Selfies with other musicians.

5. Funny, interesting or inspiring tweets from other users.

Anything you think is relevant or interesting. Try and keep it music related but if you're running low on content then posting more generic things is fine. Just make sure it's interesting and engaging. Don't just tweet for tweeting sake!
Don't be shy about asking for a retweet as well! Using #RT will greatly increase your chances of getting that pretty, pretty retweet.
Don't be afraid to tweet about the same thing twice, three times or even four times. Sometimes your tweet may get lost in users newfeeds so tweet about the same things again at a different time.
Remember even if you've only got one video. You can create lots of little bits of smaller content by documenting the process.

E.G. A picture of you guys at a meeting discussing video ideas, on the set live footage of the video being shot or even just you getting ready for it.
All of these can provide you with a few tweets worth of content to share.

How To Tweet

Posting A Tweet On Your Homepage
This tweet will appear in the newsfeeds of your followers and in the hashtag you use.
In the top right hand corner of your twitter screen there should be a blue button saying 'Tweet'. Click this button and another screen should come up where you can compose your tweet.
Once you have written your tweet press the 'Tweet' button in this new screen to send your tweet.
It's that simple.
There should be a 'Media' button on this screen also. Clicking this will allow you to attach photos or short videos.

Posting A Tweet On Other Users Walls

To tweet somebody else you can use two methods.
1. You can click the 'Tweet' button and when the new screen pops up start the tweet off with that person's twitter handle.
E.G. '@Beyonce LOVE your new track!'

Once you've composed your tweet just press the 'Tweet' button.
OR
2. You can go to that user's homepage and just under their Bio there should be a button that says 'Tweet To' which will open up another screen and allow you to write out your tweet.

Tweet Etiquette

A well composed tweet usually follows this formula.

Informative or engaging message + hashtags # + media or links

E.G. 'New Single Out Now! Hope you enjoy it. Lots of blood, sweat and tears. Please give it a retweet #RT #debutsingle #hardwork * Insert iTunes link *'
Now that was a little over 140 characters but you get the picture. Try and keep it personal, give them useful information, hashtag and attach media.
Tweets with pictures also do better so if you can attach a relavant picture then do so. People like visuals.

Stockpile Content

Getting together a stockpile of content can really help you out in the long run with twitter. Leaving it last minute and trying to find content quickly can sometimes be quite stressful and time consuming so if you can, stockpile content and steadily release it.

Pace Yourself

Twitter isn't a race. Try not to rush ahead in the pursuit of millions and millions of followers. Twitter imposes new regulations on a regular basis to try and make your growth on twitter more organic and social.
They aren't great fans of aggressive following and can sometimes penalize you, so take your time. Keep building up your targeted following but don't go overboard. Slow and steady. That's how you'll win the twitter race.

Chapter 2 – Tweepi (Follow)

What is Tweepi?

Tweepi is a website that allows you to mass follow people on twitter. Why is this helpful? Because like I've said above most users will follow someone who has followed them so you can really boost your followers pool by doing this.

Now we wont just be following everyone and anyone. We will be specifically targeting people who we think might be interesting in the music we're trying to promote.

There are some rules and regs with tweepi and twitter following but it's an invaluable tool in todays music marketing world...AND it's free! They put the free option in very small print when you sign up but keep looking and you'll be able to access this great service free of charge.

Head over to Tweepi.com now and get signed up.

Tweepi Rules and Regulations

Firstly here are some rules. Tweepi sets certain limits on how many users you can follow in a day and once you've followed that amount they will time you out until 24 hours later when you can resume your following.

Currently as of Feb 2016 on a free account you're allowed to follow 250 people a day. That's not that many so that's why we have to make every follow count and target the people we're following.

Twitter Rules and Regulations

The two limits to really take note of are the 'Daily Follow Limit' and the 'Account-based' limit.

Daily Follow Limit

This always you to follow only 1000 users per day. You can go ahead and follow more than the 250 that tweepi allows. Either by using a similar tweepi service or manually following but as I've said twitter has clamped down massively on people who go beyond these limits to don't go too mental with that follow button.

Account Based Limit

When you've followed 5000 users twitter will impose a limit on how many you can follow (Total). The algorithm may change but a general rule of thumb is once you've FOLLOWED 5000 users you can only follow up to 10% of your amount of FOLLOWERS.

E.G. 6000 people follow you then you can follow upto 6600.

This is one of the reasons we want to be picky so that most of the people we target follow back and we can continue to follow higher volumes of people.

Target Audience

Who are your fans? Who is going to like what you're producing? Take a little time to think on this and write out a fact file on what you think your typical fan is like.

Here are some characteristics to think about.

1. Music Tastes

2. Age Range

3. Gender

4. Location

5. Hobbies

6. Profession / Education

7. Fashion Sense

These are just a few to get you started and once you get a better idea of who you're selling to you can begin targeting them with your following.

Targeted Following

Once you have done your fact file and have an idea of your target audience it's time to think about successful singers, bands or musicians that are already appealing to that audience.

Think about the music you're selling and try to find atleast three artists that you feel are similar to your in sound and style.

Once you have your three artists we'll begin following their followers in the hopes they will follow you back. Because they're following someone who is quite similar to you it's probable that they're already going to like the music you're doing and become YOUR fans.

This is the main secret to success on twitter and in the music industry in general. Finding the users that want what you're selling and getting your content/product in front of them.

Get targeting.

Get following.

How To Follow and the Tweepi 'Follow All' Button

Once you sign up and log in to Tweepi you can click on the 'Dashboard' tab and you will be taken to a different screen where all of tweepi's tools are at your disposal.

We're looking for the 'Follow Followers' function.

Once you click it and go through to the next screen you'll require the twitter handle of one of your three artists. Type in their handle and click the 'Search' button.

This will then bring up all of that person's followers in pages of 20 (more if you have a paid account) and information about them.

Here are a few of the parameters it shows you

1. When They Last Tweeted

2. How Many Followers They Have

3. The Ratio Of How Many People They Follow In Relation To How Many People Follow Them Back

4. How Many Status' They Have

It's here that you can begin following but let me give you another tool to speed up this process.

Tweepi Bulk Follow Button

There's a little add on you can download for google chrome that allows you to follow an entire page of users with just one click. Just google 'Tweepi Bulk Follow Button' to find it.

Filter Criteria

Now let's filter! You can set specific criteria, which get rid of users from the page. Here are the ones that will help you find those that will be most likely to follow back and engage with you on twitter.

Last Tweeted - This shows you when a user tweeted last. If they've not tweeted in a long time then it hints towards inactivity so lets hide these users by clicking the 'Add Criteria' button.

Set to
* Last tweeted > is newer than > 5 - 7days *

Follow Ratio – This ratio is the amount of people they follow against their total number of followers. It's given in percentage. If someone has 100% follow ratio then they follow everyone that follows them.
If it's lower than 100% then they are following more people than they have followers.
If it's higher than 100% then they have more followers than they are following.
We don't really want to follow the people with over 100% as it's very unlikely they are going to follow back.

Set to
* Follow ratio > is less than > 101 *

Followers Count – This shows exactly how many followers they have. Now if someone has only a few followers I tend to get rid of them. If this person can only get my tweet to 3 people then I'll save that follow on tweepi for someone with a wider network of followers.

Set to
* Followers count > is greater than > 50-150 *

Status Count (Optional) – This shows how many status' this person has posted. If they've been online for a year and have only posted twice then best to cut them and add someone more active.

Set to
* Statuses count > is greater than > 20-30 *

Now that you know the process get following. You can add other criteria and be more selective if you wish but the above criteria should get you a good yield of followers who are ready to retweet, like and comment.
In the next chapter we'll cover the other side of this process to ensure maximum efficiency.

Chapter 3 Statusbrew.com + Friendorfollow.com (Unfollow)

Basics of Unfollowing – Because of the twitter limits we want to make sure that we don't have any people sitting in our follow list that aren't going to follow back so we have to do a little maintenance and unfollow them to keep things efficient.

These sites above are just the ones that I use but there are several others out there you can use. Depending on how much time you want to put into it you can join 4-5 of these sites to clear out your follow list. Just google 'Twitter unfollow' and use whichever one suits you best. Some give better data than others but essentially all you need is to be able to put them in chronological order.

Link for Statusbrew.com
Link for Friendorfollow.com

Who To Unfollow

After a couple of days if someone hasn't followed you back then unfollow them. On Statusbrew there's a tool kit on the side that allows you to filter the results. Just put the data in chronological order and then unfollow the users who are the oldest.

It's as simple as that.

There's also usually an option to see all those who have unfollowed you. Get rid of these too unless they're a valuable source of content in your field.

Limits

Statusbrew allows you to unfollow 100 users per day. All these sites have a similar limit so this is why I recommend using a few unfollow sites to clear your follow list so you can avoid the twitter limit until absolutely necessary.

Chapter 4 Socialoopmh + Statusbrew (Automate)

Automating Your Online Life – This is a great time saving tool and means you don't have to stop whatever you're doing at commuting hours and upload a tweet. You can have all your social media for the week done with an hour or a few hours and then you just let it run.

Link for Socialoopmh.com

Schedule Tweets - Socialoopmhs free version allows you to schedule basic tweets. This could change by the time you read this but last time I'd used it I couldn't have an image or media attached to the tweet.
It comes with a handy little URL shortener and a purging system to clean up your Inbox as well.
Auto DM or Tweet – Statusbrews' free version offers you an automating service that allows you to send someone a welcome message or tweet. These can be very useful...or they can come off really annoying. Whatever you send try and engage the fan. Don't just spam them.

Ask them a question. Get to know them a little better. I've often put up welcome messages saying I'm taking musical requests which will be uploaded to youtube and the response to those is really good.

You can run a competition. Post a snippet of your new song and the person with the best suggestion will win. The song will be called that and they will get a mention either on the album contributors or on the song itself.

Whatever it is you use just make sure it is a conversation starter and not just you mindlessly trying to flog something to them.

Free Versions VS Professional – Both of these sites have upgraded memberships which offer more advanced data, tool kits and functionality. It's up to you if you want to invest but keep it free for when you're starting. Just so you can get to grips with it before investing any money.

Conclusion

Thank you again for downloading this book!
I hope this book was able to help you to get your head around music marketing through twitter.
Just remember to engage your fans. Treat them as special and they'll be loyal. Target follow, purge and unfollow and tweet greatness. Those are my orders.
Finally, if you enjoyed this book pretty please can you leave an honest review. I'd really appreciate it.

Thank you and good luck!

Preview Of Another One Of My Music Books 'Songwriting : Powerful Melody, Lyrics and Composing Skill To Help You Craft A Hit, Find Your Voice and Become An Incredible Songwriter

The Hook

Put very simply the hook is a catchy little motif that's usually repeated throughout the song. There can be more than one but it's up to you to research your genre and see what is standard practice.

Types of Electronic Dance music may consist of two vocal hooks and nothing else whereas folk may only have one hook and the rest of the time it's about story and verses.

Most often the main hook is found in the chorus, which is usually always the most singable part of a song.

Even though repetition is key sometimes too much can annoy listeners but you can combat this by either varying the music around the vocal.

E.G. Having the first chorus stripped back and sparse and then filling out the second chorus with more instruments. Alternatively you can change the vocal melody.

E.G. If you had a double chorus towards the end of the song you could sing the first chorus down an octave to give some variation and then take it back up for the last chorus.

Having a bridge can help break things up a little as it allows you the chance to offer new melodic and lyrical content. For instance you could develop one of the minor hooks from somewhere else in the song and make it the main focus so the listeners can hear the 'new' hook in a new light and not be battered by the original hook over and over again.

Writing A Catchy Hook - These are the things that are going to get stuck in your listeners head (hopefully) so pay attention. There are some standards and convention when it comes to writing a catchy melody and you've heard them time and time again throughout your life.
In order to craft a catchy melody the quickest method I've found is to sing an already written 'catchy' hook over a track and analyze why it works.
Is it short and snappy? A long held high note? A certain melodic riff that is easy enough for most people to sing?.
What I recommend is using an already proven hook and then modifying it (Changing the melody somewhat and rewriting the lyrics completely).
This can make some songwriters squirm at the thought of using others peoples work for inspiration but in honesty we've had the same notes for hundreds of years. Over all that time, melodies and chords have probably been used in every different combination there is and certain ideas and patterns have been repeated and become convention...because they work.
Don't go stealing people's work! If you really want to be a songwriter you have to have put in effort and craft something that is authentic and as close to you as possible.

Respect and learn from those who have come before you as they've already succeeded in doing what you want to accomplish.

Melody First Approach (Vocals) – Remember when a song came out and you loved it instantly? Remember how you listened to it over and over again? Remember how you might not have known all the words but you knew every note? Melody is powerful.

Lyrics are very important too but Melody is often what stays with the listener initially and 'sticks in their head.' One of the other reasons I recommend this approach is that crafting a strong hook is very important but if you're changing the melody around a lot in order to accommodate the lyrics you might find the hook gets quite jumbled or too rhythmic.

Look at it as a challenge. You firstly set the amount of notes you're going to use and then that's the amount of syllables you have to get across your main theme.

You are free to try it the other way round but just make sure not to get too wordy. You want the majority of your words to have a strong impact and move the story along but it's a fine balance.

Voice – Know the voice you're writing for. You need to know it's range, power and tone. If you're writing for yourself I always recommend getting some vocal training to help improve your voice. Here's a course that has worked for me. It can be a bit expensive but will offer you a voice you never knew you could have.

Singing Success - www.singingsuccess.com/products

Some common problems that come up are range issues. Now if you start vocal training properly you should find your range improving to a point where you don't need to think about this too much. If you are just at the beginning of training or writing for someone else you'll need to know the limitations of their voice.

Range – Don't write it too high or too low. Even though you might love the melody. If the singer can't sing it currently then it's better to have a different melody executed well then a failed attempt.

Bridges – This is an area of the voice where the singer might experience flipping from chest voice to head voice. It's in slightly different places for each singer. Learn where this is and write around it.

Power – If the singer has problems accessing their 'Mix', belt or powerful head voice then be aware of that. They probably wont be able to deliver a huge Aretha Franklin Style note but that doesn't mean you can't write a great song for them. Write for the other strengths they have in their voice.

Flexibility – If the singer hasn't learned to move through their voice too smoothly then don't write a melody that jumps about quickly.

Check Out My Other Books

Here's some of my other musical books for you. There will be many more coming soon so look out for them.

Songwriting : Powerful Melody, Lyric and Composing Skill To Help You Craft A hit, Find Your Voice and Become An Incredible Songwriter

If the links do not work, for whatever reason, you can simply search for these titles on the Amazon website to find them.